THOUGHT &
EMOTION

POCKET EDITION

Published from
Mardukite Borsippa HQ, San Luis Valley, Colorado
Mardukite Academy & Systemology Society
for spiritual or educational purposes only

THOUGHT & EMOTION

Systemology
Professional Course
Booklet #2

Developed by Joshua Free
for the Systemology Society

© 2023, JOSHUA FREE

ISBN : 978-1-961509-26-9

Pocket Paperback Edition — *November 2023*

mardukite.com

Learn How To Let Your Spirit Fly...
Then Chart Your Flight For Ascension!

Unlock your ultimate spiritual potential by removing barriers to your true native state.

Learn how to easily attain Self-actualization and help to actualize others along the way.

A greater appreciation and understanding of *Spiritual Life* and *Existence* awaits you. Expand your reach to achieve your dreams.

Each 'Professional Course' lesson-booklet offers simple exercises and techniques that directly apply the philosophy of Systemology, assisting to increase your true knowingness, improve your capabilities in this life, and even decide what you will do in your next.

At the Mardukite Academy of Systemology, the 'Professional Course' lessons in this series are presented to Seeker's that have completed the 'Basic Course', previously released as six lesson-booklets, or the six-in-one single volume edition "Fundamentals of Systemology."

This all new presentation of the Systemology 'Pathway-to-Ascension' takes Seekers and continuing students from "Zero" to "Infinity" at lightning-fast speeds!

Discover Who You Really Are...
Because You Were Never Human

TABLET OF CONTENTS

PROFESSIONAL
COURSE
INTRODUCTION

WELCOME, SEEKER!
LET'S CHART YOUR JOURNEY
ON THE PATHWAY

Systemology is a "holistic" approach to understanding the human experience. It is not actually a singular "subject" in itself, but rather, a new way in which to view the many subjects of *Life* and all *Existence.*

This is a professional course in *Systemology*—specifically, how to *apply* the spiritual philosophy of *Mardukite Systemology* as a personal *"Pathway" to Ascension.* Our *Systemology* is a new approach to *"Self-Actualization."* It is completely relevant for the modern age and the future; and quite different from any previous similar attempts, or other traditions, you might find. What's more: it is applicable to anyone with any background.

This *"Professional Course"* series of lessons (booklets) immediately follows the material given in the *"Basic Course"* series—available as six separate pocket-sized booklets, or in a single hardcover volume titled: *"Fundamentals of Systemology: A New Thought For The 21st Century."*

This is a *new* presentation of *Systemology*, emphasizing the application of our philosophy for those *Seekers* that are *"Flying-Solo"*—or else working through their studies and exercises as solitary practitioners. This is a new innovation for *Systemology*. Aside from the book *"Crystal Clear,"* all of our former advanced courses have placed a focus on *"Traditional Piloting"*—where experienced practitioners assist *Seekers* in *"processing."*

To receive the greatest benefit from this study: it is expected that a *Seeker* will already be familiar with the fundamental concepts and terminology (previously relayed in the *Basic Course*) before using lessons from the *Professional Course*. This will allow us to cover the extensive territory of the *Pathway* much more quickly. However, for reference, a basic "*glossary*" of vocabulary used in this lesson is provided in the "*appendix*."

A NEW VIEW OF THE HUMAN SPIRIT

Systemology is not a religion and does not require any type of *faith*. It is, however, built upon a "spiritual" premise—and as such is an "applied spiritual philosophy." It is based on ancient teachings that we are *Spiritual Beings* essentially "wearing" bodies like clothes—or using them as "vehicles." Yet our true native nature is not *physical*, but beyond this existence; and we can certainly operate a "body" from *outside* of it.

We are **all** *Spiritual Beings*—each of us a *unit* of *Spiritual Awareness*—that have experienced a very long *Spiritual Timeline* of existence. Although we might be particularly attached to the familiar "physical shells" associated with *this* lifetime, our true *"Spiritual Lifetime"* is seemingly *eternal*. We have been many things before *Human*, and we go onward as a *Spiritual Being* after our *"genetic vehicle"* of *this* incarnation perishes.

While a "spiritual" view of the *Human Condition* may not seem unique to our philosophy, just how often is the concept treated *systematically*? For that matter: just how many people, supposedly raised to this or that religion, or professing to believe one thing or another, actually live their lives as though they are *Spirits?*

As *Spiritual Beings* of immortal existence and infinite potential, we are not simply the *"creations"* of an even greater *Being-*

ness; we are, in fact, an integral part of that *"creative force"* which permeates all existence.

Our basic nature is to be a *"creative be-ing"*—our highest goals are *"to create."* And as such a being—which we refer to as an *Alpha-Spirit* in *Systemology*—we have run into some difficulties along the course of our *Spiritual Timeline* and found ourselves trapped within material *Universes* of our own collaborative *creation.*

Since we did not start out our existence in a trapped condition, it is correct to say that we have *"fallen"* from our native *"godlike"* states. It did not happen all at one, but progressively and systematically. We know our "troubles" have resulted from accumulated "barriers" and "block-ages"—or *fragmentation*—during our vast experiences as *Spiritual Beings.* They are not because we lack something; but be-cause of what's been added.

In *Systemology*, we systematically examine those routes by which we must have descended to reach our present condition, then reverse the direction of travel and chart a personal *"Pathway to Ascension."* Of course, the exact "details" of the *Spiritual Timeline* will be different for each individual *Seeker*. However, we have been able to systematically chart our *Pathway* based on common patterns of *Human fragmentation.*

In the most basic terms: the *fragmentation* that defines our "downward spiral" consists of decisions or considerations where we deny our true nature. This includes those decisions to *"withdraw"* rather than *"reach"*; where we choose to *not-know* rather than *know*; to *not-communicate* rather than *communicate*; and ultimately, to take *no-responsibility* for being a *creative-cause*, and therefore succumb to being an *effect*.

But there is *hope!* And much more importantly: there is an effectively workable *way out* of the mazes and traps of our existence. If you are reading this now, you have already begun to gather your tools and build up the *"horsepower"* necessary to break the gravity holding your *Spiritual Beingness* to the *Human Condition*.

STUDYING THE
PROFESSIONAL COURSE

Most *Seekers* study and practice *Systemology* at-a-distance and independent of the "Mardukite Academy" or any "Master-level" mentors trained therein. This means that the *books* (and to a lesser degree, the *internet*) are the only means of direct contact a *Seeker* maintains with the "Systemology Society" during their studies. A continuing *Seeker* from the *"Basic Course"* will be familiar with the style of study found in *this* course.

Misunderstood words are the most common reason an individual abandons studying a subject. When a misunderstanding occurs, *Awareness* declines. These misunderstandings start to "stack up" after the first occurrence, and as a result, the level of interest and attention will also decline. This is how a "confusion" develops; and the individual will get "bored" with the subject, feel tired, and unable to concentrate.

One solution is to return to the part of the material that was still interesting and enjoyable to read. When scanning around that area of text, there is likely to be a new word (or new specific use of a familiar word) that is unclear, but was passed by unnoticed. All *Systemology* books include their own *glossary*. Using this *glossary* and a high-quality dictionary will help resolve this misunderstanding once it is located.

An effective education of any subject is taught on a *gradient*. This is what is intended by presenting the study of something as "*grades*." Rather than treating a subject as one total mass, true learning is achieved by increasing one's understanding with a *gradual* increase upward. The *ascent* to a mountaintop is not successfully achieved in one leap, but by targeting and reaching specific checkpoints along the way.

This *Professional Course* consists of a series of lessons (booklets) that gradually increase a *Seeker*'s ability to understand and apply the practices and techniques of *Systemology* as a complete "*Pathway to Ascension*." It is an appropriate study for continuing *Seekers* (from the *Basic Course*), but also "advanced" *Systemologists*.

Each lesson (booklet) of the *Professional Course* applies *Systemology* to a particular subject (or focus). It is best if the entire course can be studied and applied in sequential order. These lessons also employ a style of practice or technique called "*Systematic Processing*." An introduction to applying this methodology is provided in the final lesson (booklet) of the *Basic Course*—or in the "*Fundamentals of Systemology*" volume.

To study the *Professional Course* just like a student at the Academy: a *Seeker* reads through all instructional material and applies each exercise (or "*process*") presented in the text to the extent they comfortably can, before continuing on to the next lesson (booklet).

When first starting on the *Pathway* as a *Solo* practitioner, without the aid of an experienced *Pilot*, a *Seeker* shouldn't "push too hard" or allow themselves to get too "stuck" on any one area (lesson) or *process*. It is not expected that any one area will be completely handled when first introduced. For optimum results, it is expected that a serious *Seeker* will make more than one "pass" through the entire *Professional Course*.

The *Professional Course* is not altogether different from other forms of practical or technical education: where the instruction and exercises are delivered to a completion, and then a student further increases their abilities, strength and skill-level by applying additional practice throughout their life. Therefore, a student should not concern themselves with perfectly mastering each step (or lesson) before progressing forward.

Additional passes through the material are likely to result in different *"realizations"* (an increased *level of understanding*) than a previous time. New "layers" of *Knowingness* may now be accessible during a *process* that may not have been before. It is important to avoid invalidating

the progress you've made just because
one area is not completely handled right
away, or if a certain *process* seems too difficult on the first pass.

CHARTING A COURSE ON
THE PATHWAY

Although we can communicate a systematic structure to *fragmentation,* the personal journey experienced along the *Pathway*
will be different for each *Seeker.* For example, certain areas will seem more "*turbulent*" or difficult for one *Seeker* than
another. We tend to say that these areas
have more "*charge*" on them—or that
they are more "*heavily charged.*" It is best
to handle such areas when you are
already feeling "good" and not in a situation (or condition) where that specific
area is consistently being "*triggered*" or
"*restimulated.*"

As an applied philosophy, *Systemology* "theory" can be easily utilized in the "laboratory" of the "world-at-large" in everyday life. This is implied within the basic instruction of each lesson. Unlike other "sciences" that conduct experiments by making a change to some "objective variable" *out there* and waiting to see an effect, our focus is the individual (or *Observer*) themselves, and how *they* affect the "*Reality*" perceived.

In addition to applying *Systemology* "New Thought" to everyday life, our philosophy is applied by using specific exercises and systematic techniques. These "*processes*" provide the most stable personal gain (and *realizations*) for each area; but only when actually applied with a *Seeker's* full "*presence*" and *Awareness*.

This *Professional Course* is designed so that it may be easily read and studied with little concern for what "dangers" these teachings—or *processing*—might unleash. However, there are still some guidelines that pertain to the "best-uses" of these course lessons, particularly if a *Seeker* intends for stable development.

Skipping over too much material/*processing* in early lessons may make attempts to understand (or apply) later lessons more difficult. However, once the complete *Professional Course* is worked through at least once in its entirety, specific areas can then be later returned to and treated with a greater sense of *Awareness* and *"presence"* than before. Of course, in *"Traditional Piloting,"* the rate of processing is monitored by an experienced practitioner; but in *"Solo-Processing,"* a *Seeker* must regulate their own progress on the *Pathway*.

Applying a systematic technique is called *"running a process."* The *processes* are designed with very simple instructions or "*command-lines*." To *run* a *processing command-line*, a *Seeker* may be assisted by the communication of that *line* from a "*Co-Pilot*" (as in "*Traditional Piloting*"). But even then, a *Seeker* must still personally "input" the *command* as *Self*. For this reason —and quite thankfully— *Solo-Processing* is possible.

TAKING FLIGHT ON THE PATHWAY

Processing Techniques are intended to treat the *Spiritual Being* or *Alpha-Spirit*; the individual themselves. It is applied by the *Alpha-Spirit*—then *Self-directed* to the "Mind-System" or even a "body" (*genetic-vehicle*), both of which are "constructs" that the *Alpha-Spirit* (*Self*, or the "I-AM" *Awareness unit*) operates, but neither of which is actually *Self*. *Fragmentation* causes *Humans* to falsely identify *Self as* the "*Mind*" or even a "*Body*."

The *Professional Course* lessons (booklets) are designed for the *Beginning Seeker* in mind—one that may have an understanding of theory, but with little experience in practice. That being said: each of these lessons may be used toward total *Beta-Defragmentation* within a specific area. There are also more *processes* given for each subject than may be necessary to achieve an *ultimate end-point realization* on that entire area.

Some *processes* can be treated quite lightly at first; others may require a bit of working at in order to get *"running"* well. It is important to set aside a period of time when you can be dedicated to your studies and *processing*. This period of time is referred to as a *"processing session."* The reason for this, is that when a *process* does start *running* well, it is important to be able to complete it to a satisfactory *"end-point."*

The purpose of *systematic processing* is to be able to *really* "look" at things and even determine the *considerations* we have made—or attitudes we have decided—about *Reality* as a result of those experiences. It doesn't do us much good to simply "glance"—or to *restimulate* something uncomfortable and then quickly *withdraw* from it once again, leaving more of our *attention* yet again behind and held fixedly on it.

Generally speaking, a *Seeker* continues to *run* a *process* so long as something is "happening"—which is to say, the *process* is still producing a change. Usually this is evident by the type of "answers" that a *command-line* helps a *Seeker* originate from the database of their own *Mind-System*. The *command-lines* do not "do" anything on their own. They assist a *Seeker* to direct their own attention toward increasing *Awareness*.

Of course, a *Seeker* may also cease to generate new "data" from a *process* without reaching an *"ultimate" realization* as an *"end-point."* It is possible that additional "layers" (or even other "areas") require handling before anything "deeper" is accessible. If this is the case, end the *process.* But, if a *Seeker* is *withdrawing* from something uncomfortable that was incited or stirred up, then a *process* is *run* until they feel "good" about it.

In case the thought of encountering *"turbulence"* is a concern: the techniques given as *"Opening Procedures"* of a *Formal Session* (in the *Basic Course*), and those found in the earliest lessons of the *Professional Course*, are quite useful when applied as "safety nets" for maintaining *Awareness* and *presence*, even when *Flying-Solo*.

One of the benefits to *Flying-Solo* is that *processing* is entirely *Self-determined*. This already provides a certain built-in "safety" for a practitioner. Anything you *restimulate* by *Self-determinism* is *your thing*. It is not incited by external *other-determined* influences (or other "source-points" in existence) that make you an *effect*. It can be more easily handled in *processing*—or you can simply let things "cool down" and come back to it again.

While it may seem "mysterious" to beginners, a *Seeker* gets a sense for knowing how long to *run* a *process* only with practice. Once you have spent some time actually applying the *Professional Course*, there are many aspects that become "second nature" because they are, in fact, a part of our true original nature. All we have done is *"reverse engineer"* the routes of *creation* and *consideration* that are already *our own*.

LESSON TWO: THOUGHT & EMOTION

NEW SYSTEMATIC PROCESSES
INTRODUCED IN THIS LESSON

- Flight-Logging (*"Session Journaling"*)
- Attitude Control (*objective process*)
- Associative Identification (*objective proc.*)
- Creating Emotions (*objective process*)
  [*"Make It Feel"*]
- Conceptual Processing (*basic alternation*)
  [*"Get The Sense Of"*]
- Automation and Reactivity
- *"Make A Copy"*
- Confronting "As-It-Is"
  [*"Sitting Face-To-Face"*]
- Subjective Processing (*general*)
- Confronting The Past
  [*"Analytical Recall"*]

EXISTING PROCEDURES
DISCUSSED IN THIS LESSON

- Beta-Awareness (*Basic Course*)
- Formal Session (*Basic Course*)
- Control of Mind-Body (*Lesson #1*)

KEEPING A FLIGHT LOG

Whether a *Seeker* is *Co-Piloted* or *Flying-Solo*, it is traditional to keep a *"Flight Log"* or *record* of the journey on the *Pathway*. This follows in line with the systematic approach of our philosophy. It is also helpful to refer to if running into any misunderstood *turbulence* along the way —such as *"underrun"* or *"overrun"* of a *process*, as described in the first lesson (booklet) of this *Professional Course*.

A *Systemologist* keeps careful records of their *"processing sessions"* and any other *realizations* that have occurred while traveling the *Pathway*. In 2020, the *Systemology Society* developed the *"Truth Seeker's Adventure Journal"* to make this easier— but you can easily use any notebook to "log" your progress if you know what information is most critical to keep track of. Be consistent.

The following is a brief list of all general information tracked in *Traditional Piloting*:

–*Name* of the *Pilot* or *Co-Pilot*;
–*Location* and *Weather*;
–*Date* and *Day of the Week*;
–*Beta-Awareness* (at *start/end* of session);
–*Time* (at *start* and *end* of session);
–*Processes*, *Routines* or *Procedures* used;
–*Terminals* (*masses, objects, people, places*) contacted/recalled/imagined in session;
–Everything a *Seeker says* in session; and
–Any *Realizations* that occur.

Records are important for optimum effectiveness and tracing any incomplete *processes* or other sources of *turbulence* that may have become accessible, where they were not before. The techniques included in the *Professional Course* series are not meant to be particularly strenuous, however, even the most basic of these *processes* can "stir up" or "trigger" various things—each of which should be handled as they *resurface*.

Another purpose for *journaling* as a standard routine is to *"extrovert"* after a session; to get all the stuff that took place down on paper, externally. This also helps keep a *Seeker* from keeping any residual attention remaining on the session and not in present space-time once the session has ended.

CONTROL OF MIND AND BODY

Thoughts (of the *"Mind"*) and subsequent *emotions* (of the *"Body"*) are under the command of the *Alpha-Spirit*. Of course, we often find ourselves relinquishing the control of these aspects to others. Sometimes it is simply a part of the roles we play—or perhaps it helps to keep things interesting—but in the end, it is always within your power to regain total control of your *thoughts* and *emotions*.

Some basic exercises in this area of "attitude control" are provided in the *Basic Course*, as is an introduction to the *Beta-Awareness Scale*. However, let us start off this lesson (booklet) with a demonstration of light *"objective processing."*

"*Choose a 'neutral' object (that you have no strong feelings about).*"

"*Look at the object.*"

"*Decide to feel various positive things about the object (that you love it, that it is beautiful to look at, that it is wonderful to have close to you, &tc).*"

"*Maintain this positive attitude for several minutes.*"

"*(Then reverse this and) Decide to feel various negative things about the object (that you despise it, that it is ugly to look at, that it is harmful to be near, &tc) and continue this for several minutes.*"

"*(Then reverse this again and) Decide to maintain a positive attitude about the object for several minutes.*"

When this *process* is practiced seriously, a *Seeker* may initially encounter some challenges in exercising their fluid alternation of attitudes back and forth. Various unintended "reactions" may also occur as one makes the decision to feel one way or another. This should be repeated several times on the same object until any automatic reaction or turbulence has "smoothed out"—or *"flattened"* as we tend to say (using *wave* terms).

Once this has been *run* and *flattened* on the same object, you may then use the *process* again on other objects in the room. Always end-off during the "positive" side of an alternating *process*, rather than the "negative." This *process* is not intended to solve all *fragmentation* preventing total control of the *Mind* and *Body*; but it is a very productive practice—and it may lead to the same *realizations* on which our theories for it are based.

ASSOCIATIVE IDENTIFICATION

Much of what *Humans* consider as *"know-ledge"* really relates to *"associative identi-fication"*—or more simply, *"association."* Entire fields of philosophy—such as *"epi-stemology"*—are dedicated to theories to explain *"how* we *know* what we *know."* *Systematic Processing* allows a *Seeker* a dir-ect approach to determining the truth of these matters for themselves.

Early work by the *Mardukite Research Org* served as a precursor to establishing the *Systemology Society*—and within that body of early research, we uncovered a significant amount of information regard-ing the control of human consciousness with *"language"* at the inception of mod-ern civilization thousands of years ago.

Most *"thinking"* involves *association*, not *Knowingness.* The type of *realizations* that occur in *processing* lead to a higher state of actual *Knowingness*. This *Knowingness* is not the result of freewheeling thought —it is not a result of "thinking about" or "figuring on" things. The systematic approach we take in *processing* is similar to natural "thought processes"—but a *Seeker* more directly is applying *attention* to actually *look* at things.

The following *process* demonstrates all of these points. When first practicing this, it is most effective to select an object present around you that has a lot of "mass" to it—such as a table, a chair, or a bookshelf, *&tc.* Then, select something else with "mass" (not present in the environment) that it would be ridiculous to associate with the object—such as an apple, a garden-hose, or a stop-sign, *&tc.*

The basic *"processing command-line"* (or "PCL") for this exercise is:

"Look at the object and immediately think of the ridiculous association you have chosen."

—or—

*"Look at the object and think of the ridiculous
association as if it were automatic."*

To be most effective, it is best if you alternate doing this with *looking* at something else around you and noticing
something about it. Then you can redirect
your *attention* back to the object you are
working with, and getting an immediate
sense that it is the ridiculous alternative
association instead.

As an advanced application, you might
try to actually *imagine* or *visualize* the intended alternative in place of the object.
When you "spot" this *imagined* alternative, make a point to *notice* specific things
about it. This will also increase the detail
or vibrancy of your *visualization*. This
may be practiced further using various
different objects in your environment and
associating other alternative ridiculous
items.

Usually we *associate* "ideas" and "concepts" in our *"thinkingness,"* but the actual substance or significance we attach to our thoughts and feelings often regards something with "mass"—which is to say, a *"terminal"* using *Systemology* vocabulary. We treat specific *terminals* more directly in later *"subjective processes."*

CREATING EMOTIONAL FLOWS

Strength and ability of an *Alpha-Spirit* is rooted in *Self-determinism*—of being *at cause*. Therefore, we find that misappropriating (or inappropriately assigning) *cause* in our life is one of the many ways in which we increasingly come to consider ourselves primarily the *effect* of others, and even the *Universe* as a whole.

It is quite customary with the *Human Condition* to assign *cause* of "ill effects" as far away from *Self* as possible. From this, we tend to "blame" others for how we think and feel. This is not to say there are not many influential factors to our experiences; but ultimately, it is *Self* that decides how to think and feel.

Whenever we "incite" or "inspire" an *emotional reaction* in another, they sometimes tell us that we *caused* them to *feel* this or that way—that *they* are experiencing the *effect* of our *presence*. Of course, many factors are likely at play here; but the ability to *create* a specific *emotion, sensation* or state of *thought* is certainly within the power of an *Alpha-Spirit*.

With *objective processing,* a *Seeker* can *knowingly* practice getting this sense of *creating* or *projecting* an "emotional flow." This will also start to familiarize a *Seeker* with the idea of more directly considering (or treating) all *energy, communication* and *attention-lines* as a "flow."

"Look around and choose an object."

"(Alternate) Make it feel happy; Make it feel sad."

When practicing this, perform the action by *intention*. You don't need to actually "say" anything—telling jokes or scolding—to produce the effect. Just get the sense of deciding upon, and intending, the idea or concept very strongly and clearly. Then, get the sense that just being in your presence makes it happen.

After this is practiced for a while on a specific object, try it on other items in the room. Once you are comfortable with this pair of states, consider other states on the *Beta-Awareness Scale* such as *"love"* and *"hate"*; then with *"interest"* and *"boredom."* Starting with the extremes will eventually allow you to easily practice with any emotion or mental state.

When we interact with the *Universe*—and other lifeforms in the *Universe*—*communications "flow"* in various directions between *terminals*. In *Systemology*, we refer to these individual *flows* as *"circuits"* — therefore *"circuits"* between *"terminals."* We adopted this terminology from the field of electronics; but, this systematic approach has allowed us to understand and apply our philosophy in *systematic processing*.

"Look around and choose an object."

"(Alternate) Get a sense of feeling sorry for the object; get a sense of the object feeling sorry for you."

Practice for a while on the same object, then pick another item and do the same. If a *Seeker* continues this long enough, the ultimate *end-point* would be a greater control over the *reactivity* associated with *"grief"* and *"sympathy."* A complete mastery is not expected with a single pass through the *Professional Course*.

This *process* may be applied to other states of *Beta-Awareness*—"fear" or *"being afraid of*"; "anger" or "*being angry at*"; "cheerfulness" or "*happy to have you/it there*"; &tc. Again, working with these states *knowingly* in *processing* should produce some sense of having a greater control over the experience of them.

AUTOMATION AND REACTIVITY

One of the principle areas of *Systemology* is the study of *automated mechanisms* and *reactivity*. In basic terms: this is how *systems* influence one another. Most systems are *dynamic*, which means that they do not exist in exclusion separately from other *systems*; thus their "*state*" may be influenced by other outside "*conditions*."

The *Alpha-Spirit* has the ability to command the control of all its *systems*—and the ability to automate that control as well. While the "*Body*" does receive its commands from various Mind-Systems, much of what is handled by the *"Mind"* takes place on *automatic*, leading *unknowingly* to act out behaviors as a *reaction*.

A systematic way of handling those tendencies of the *Human Condition* that are happening on *automatic* is to *knowingly* "exaggerate" their behavior. This is far easier than invalidating early efforts to "stop" it altogether at first. Then, in practice, you alternate doing it more and doing it less. You basically keep doing the thing *knowingly* until it seems to come more under your control.

There are many aspects of the *Human Condition* that are experienced *"on automatic,"* but this basic technique is quite effective for handling the most accessible (visible or already known) tendencies. Let's try another exercise within the same area of *processing*.

"Close your eyes."
"What are you looking at?"

Some individuals see a specific *mental image* (*visual picture*), or *energy-bursts*, or even *blackness* (but a uniquely intense *blackness*) when they close their eyes. This occurs seemingly automatically. The *process* continues:

"Make a duplicate copy of what you see (right next to it)."

However a *Seeker* manages this action is acceptable. It might be an *imagined* "holographic" duplicate; or perhaps you imagined a "screen" (as a background) to place a copy on. At first, we are really only concerned with getting a sense of this, even if the *Seeker* has difficulty with creating vivid *mental images*.

Once a single copy of whatever is seen is made next to it, make another duplicate copy on the other side. Now make more copies to the right and to the left. Don't limit the space to a linear horizon in front of you; make more copies above your head and below your feet and behind you. Then continue to the next *process*.

"*Close your eyes.*"

"*What are you looking at?*"

"*Make a mental image copy of it.*"

"*Now change its color; Turn it ---.*"

Whatever the color-quality already (or *automatically*) is, "*turn it...*" to another color. In between cycles of this *process*, be sure to open your eyes and look around your environment, spot things and notice specific points on them. This alternates using purely "mental" exercises with re-orienting *presence* in that space and time. As an advanced application, a *Seeker* creates many copies and starts changing the color of each one individually.

We have mentioned "*association*" previously in this lesson (booklet); a large amount of our *associated knowledge* is made up of "automatic" and "reactive" *mental imagery* that represents the "terminal" or "mass" that we *most* "*associate*" with that concept or piece of data. Often, this restricts us from considering a wider scope (or range) of potential possibilities.

There is another phenomenon observed in *Systemology*, referred to as a "*compulsively created mental image.*" This is otherwise called a "*stuck picture*" —one that is consistently brought to mind, or *unknowingly created*, outside of, or without, one's own *Self-determinism*. Most individuals have a few of these that are *imprints* of incidents and past experiences. More often then not, a "*stuck picture*" is of something unpleasant.

For example: if you are worried about something, there is often a "*mental image*" representing whatever you are worried about that is "*stuck in your mind*" —which is to say, that you can't stop thinking about. The systematic solution is to make many copies of the "*stuck picture*" —first changing its color, then altering the entire nature of the imagery one part at a time until the whole "scenery" comes under your control.

"Look around (the room) and spot an object."

"What thought comes to mind?"

"Make a duplicate copy of the thought."

"Make another copy (make many copies, thinking it many times)."

"(Alternate) Make the thought 'louder'; Make the thought 'quieter'."

Having the nature and intensity of thoughts under your control will assist in better handling those aspects and items we'd rather not *confront*.

CONFRONTING "AS-IT-IS"

The word *"confront"* has many negative connotations in modern language. For example, we tend to refer to someone who is quick to exhibit anger with others as *confrontational*. But this only partly demonstrates the true meaning of the word, which is: "to come around to the front"—or "come around to face."

In some ways, we have been lightly (but directly) "*confronting*" objects, emotions, and states of mind throughout this lesson. We have demonstrated that control over our experience of something, lies not in our avoidance or withdrawal, but our willingness to *look* at it "*As-It-Is.*"

The first basic *confront processes* (also known as "*concentering*" in archaic "*New Thought*" traditions) are important, but easily dismissed or incorrectly performed. The ability to properly *confront* existence "*As-It-Is*"—and free of automatic-associations and other reactivity—is a critical component to the *Pathway*. But, this does not take place all at once, just as the "blockage" to this native ability did not always seem as solid.

When we *look* at something *"As-It-Is,"* we are *confronting* it. The ability to do this in *Self-Honesty*—without those *associations* and *reactivity*—is a practiced skill, one that improves the further along the *Pathway* one progresses.

Not unlike states sought through traditional forms of *"meditation,"* to *confront,* we practice by simply *looking* at something with all of our *presence* and *attention* without any *distraction*—either from the *"Body,"* the environment, or thoughts. This also increases personal ability to provide *presence* and focus *attention.*

There is an archaic *Tibetan* tradition of *"Sitting Face-to-Face"* which a *Seeker* may practice best with a partner. This is performed by simply sitting across from another person without talking or giving in to reactions. In *session,* this may be practiced with an object. What is important is to be able to "extrovert" your *attention*; to project it to a point that is outside and away from where you *perceive* the *"Body"* or *"Mind"* to be located.

Unlike the previous *process*—where we "make a copy" of distractions (thoughts and emotions) to practice getting them under our control—this exercise is not concerned with addressing each distraction as a *thing*, but rather ignoring them and refocusing *attention* exactly where you want it. Much may "stir up" in the *"Body"* and *"Mind"* just by sitting quietly maintaining eye contact with someone.

If any discomfort, emotional reactions or intruding thoughts "stir up" or "turn on" while performing this *process*, simply maintain focus of your *attention* "outwards" until they "simmer down" or "turn off." There are many times in *Life* when you need to persist or handle something in spite of distractions, and the ability to do this *clearly* without losing *focus*, is an important skill for optimum *survival* (and our ability to *create*).

This may be practiced until you are able to achieve these results effortlessly for a few minutes at will. Afterward, reapplying the *"Control of Mind-Body"* process used in the *"Opening Procedures"* of a *Formal Session* (and reintroduced in *Lesson-1* of this series) may yield different results. The PCL for this is:

"Put all of your attention on the upper back corners of the room; Keep your attention there and ignore all distractions."

INTRODUCING
SUBJECTIVE PROCESSING

The sequential *Pathway to Ascension* relayed in this *Professional Course* series of lessons (booklets) begins with a lot of *"objective universe processing."* This means those *processes* which mainly *"extrovert"* *attention,* or focus it *"external"* to the *"Body"* on the *"objective"* *Universe.* Even when treating something *"internal"* (like emotion and thought), we have, up until now, *processed* a *"projection"* of it into *"external"* objects.

The majority of *processing* used on the *Pathway* concerns the *"subjective universe"* of the individual themselves. This might be best understood as a *Seeker's* own *"Personal Universe."* However, all of the previous *processes* allow for early personal development, are excellent demonstrations of *Systemology,* and quite useful for realigning full *presence* in between long periods of "introverted" *subjective processing.*

Conceptual Processing is a form of *subjective-universe processing* because it asks a *Seeker* to "consider," "conceive," or "get the sense of" a concept being (or not being) a certain way, in spite of how it might really appear or manifest in this *objective-universe* (that is otherwise agreed to as *"Reality"* for all concerned).

55

Since *subjective-universe processing* is such an integral part of the remaining *Professional Course* series, it is important that we introduce it, and its systematic application, in the earliest lessons. There is also some additional instruction that is necessary, which a *Seeker* should combine with what they've already learned about *systematic processing* in general. This is important for *Flying-Solo* without experienced assistance.

Systematic Processing is *not* a form of meditation or psychotherapy; and it most certainly *isn't* freewheeling thought, where an individual just skips from one thought to another or lingers compulsively on one. Our methods originally developed from a need within the *Mardukite Research Organization* to provide *Seekers* with an effective form of ministerial counseling or spiritual advisement. *Systemology* developed thereafter.

When working *Solo,* it does not help to

start "spinning in" on endless cycles of *"thinkingness"* that ultimately leave you more confused, or at the very least, less certain, of your ability and your progress on the *Pathway*. It is *certainty*, and the brighter "feel good" *objective processes*, that will help carry you through the rough spots.

To avoid stimulating anything significant, we will introduce *subjective processing* with a "neutral" example that would not otherwise appear in a *session* and should not have any mental *"charge"* or emotional turbulence attached to it.

A *Pilot* gives (or a *Seeker* reads) the PCL: *"Think of a Fruit."* Now, the *Seeker* would either communicate (or write down) all the *"answers"* that come to mind from this. The two-way communication (or writing, if *Solo*) assists in keeping a *Seeker* from getting too introverted or "spun-in" on a *subjective process*.

At first, in this example, a *Seeker* might have to orient themselves, or internally *process* the *command-line* for a moment, and then the initial "*answer*" (or "*response*" to the mental inquiry) might be "a cherry." And so, this would be communicated (or written) the moment it comes into mind. This also allows that cycle to get acknowledged, and the *Seeker* is free to come up with another *answer*. Soon, many of them start to occur quite easily. The *end-point* here is when you feel good about "*thinking of fruits.*"

If this were a *process* regarding something with *fragmentation* attached to it, there would initially be some noticeable difficulty or resistance in *running* the PCL—or the "*answers*" wouldn't make sense, or would be about something else. *Systematic Processing* increases a *Seekers* "certainty" in being able to push through the "mental barriers" and regain control of "emotional turbulence."

An example of *fragmentation* if *processing* our example, would include "spinning-in" on free-thought that concerns the nature, or definition, of what a *"fruit"* is, *&tc.* This is one of the reasons an experienced *Pilot* will make certain that a *Seeker* fully understands the words used in a PCL before using it in *processing*.

Free-thought, or freewheeling thought, is what takes place due to *associations* and unfocused *attention*. For example: a *Seeker* answers (or writes) "a cherry" and then starts (internally) asking themselves questions about "cherry-pies," which leads to wondering if they are hungry, and so on. This is not *processing*. This does nothing to *flatten* the *"wave,"* *"charge"* (or *"turbulence"*) of the *fragmentation* presenting itself.

When *running* a *process*, you want to focus on getting direct *responses* or *answers* to the PCL; even if it's not posed as a "question" outright. This is what makes our work a *systematic process*; because you are *looking* at *responses* or *answers* from a "computational databank." These are not random *responses*, but *answers* that result from *systematic processing* taking place "internally" in the "*Mind*" due to *running* our intended PCL.

During a *process*, the PCL is the query or question, which already puts a *Seeker* in some degree of *uncertainty*. The key to *running* a *process* is to then produce *responses* or *answers*, not pose more questions to yourself. If you consider each PCL in a "*What is..?*" form, you should be most focused on "*It is...*" answers.

BASIC SUBJECTIVE PROCESSING

To further illustrate the application and proper *running* of *subjective processing*, we will begin with a few light examples that are real *processes*. Alternating *command-*

lines may be designated "A" and "B" (or however many steps there are to the *process*. These can be *logged* in a journal simply by putting the letters at the top of the page and using each subsequent line to keep track of the appropriate list. Therefore:

A. *"Think of something you wouldn't mind remembering. (What is it?)"*

B. *"Think of something you wouldn't mind forgetting. (What is it?)"*

This is systematically more effective than simply drilling on one consideration repeatedly. A *process* is already *run* in repetition, but doing this with *subjective processing* also allows you to realign your focus and avoid getting "spun-in" or "off-track" on some additional cycle of thought.

There are also *subjective processes* where you do simply keep listing *"answers"* from one PCL until one seems right—but that is only used when you are scouting for a specific *"answer"* and not unraveling a whole chain of *considerations.* This type of work will be treated later on in the *Professional Course* series.

In *running* our present example, you may find that answers do not immediately present themselves, but eventually they do—and at one point, perhaps quite quickly. There will then be a point when new answers don't seem to be occurring and suddenly the *process* seems difficult. The *realization* or improvement will usually come by pushing through this at least once, *looking* a bit "deeper" to see if there is something else.

"What is something you agree with?"
"What is something you disagree with?"

Using *subjective processing* for *defragmentation* generally consists of "freeing up" *considerations* that may otherwise be rigidly fixed in place as they are. This rigidity or solidity produces what we may refer to as a *"stuck flow"*—which is fixed continuously in one direction. The systematic solution to this is to practice an *alternation* of *consideration* from multiple sides or angles. Without understanding this, some of our *processing* would be seen as counter-intuitive. For example:

"Decide that something is important."
"Decide that something is unimportant."

In *running* this, we aren't as much concerned with what that "something" is for a single *process*, or what the *Seeker* ultimately feels about it. The entire purpose is to practice *considering* that something *is* or *isn't*. As a result, an individual is more certain in their ability to actually "change their minds" of their own choosing.

For the final example in this section, separate your journal page into four columns —A, B, C, and D—and just think about something related to the categories given for each PCL. For each PCL, you will think about something and then list what *"it is"* as if responding to the follow up query of *"What is it?"* The answers are not as important as the practice of maintaining *Self-determined* control over your thoughts.

A. *"Think about Space."*

B. *"Think about Time."*

C. *"Think about Energy."*

D. *"Think about Matter."*

CONFRONTING THE PAST

Most of the *processing* presented in the *Professional Course* series will target specific areas. This is important for learning the various *processes* and *techniques,* and also for developing *certainty* and increased *Awareness* for when a *Seeker* cycles through the material of the entire course additional times.

Stable progress on the *Pathway*—and *processing sessions* in general—results from being able to handle (or *process*) whatever presents itself. A *Seeker* learns to *confront* rather than *withdraw* from their own *Mind.* But before that can happen, it is necessary to have *certainty* on the right *processes* to apply to the right situation.

Fragmentation is an accumulation of debris or blockage that occurs gradually over time. As our spiritual philosophy relays, the individual (or *Seeker*) as an *Alpha-Spirit* has been around for a very long time. It has followed its own path of existence as an *Awareness* that we refer to as a "*Spiritual Timeline.*"

The *Spiritual Timeline* extends like a "track"—and it includes all of our "*past*" existences (as an *Awareness*) far and beyond *this* physical incarnation (lifetime), or even *this* Universe. We presume that it extends well afterward into what we would consider the *future* as well. The part which is *"past,"* we call the *"Back-track."*

We have mentioned *"stuck pictures"* and *"stuck flows"* or other rigidly fixed forms of *fragmentation* that limit our total potential and range of *considerations*. These actually accumulate as "energetic-masses" on our *Backtrack*. We often refer to these masses as *"imprints"* when they are *associated* with a specific *incident* or *terminal*. The more *imprints* accumulate, the more *fragmented* the experience of *Life* and *Existence* becomes.

Eventually, to fully *Self-Actualize* for *Ascension*, an individual needs to *clear* the channels of *fragmentation*, particularly those that include *"past trauma."* If *Flying-Solo*, the best course of action is not to simply *fly* headlong straight into the trauma, but instead, to first build up *certainty* and *inertia* (or else, personal *horsepower*) with the basic *processes* — and *recalling* pleasant times to balance-out handling of the unpleasant.

To conceptualize the *Backtrack*, think of a long reel of "movie film" that is systematically categorized with various dates and incidents—along with the *considerations* that we made as a result of those events. An individual (*Alpha-Spirit*) is as well off as they have full *Awareness* on the contents of their own *Backtrack*.

Those energetic-masses that accumulate actually block our clear view of the *Spiritual Timeline* or *Backtrack* and inhibit us from experiencing and handling better recall of the data. Although *attention units* of our *Awareness* are entangled up in the compulsive unknowing creation of these *imprints*, our resistance to wanting to *look* at them eventually turns into automatic tendencies that provide us only "*blackness*" to see.

Obviously, our existence has not only

consisted of unpleasant experiences—and it is on these that we should put our attention in order to reduce any *"blackness"* that is associated with our history, in this lifetime or otherwise. When *Flying-Solo* without assistance of an experienced *Pilot* (or *Co-Pilot*), *use* *recall* of "pleasant memories" if handling past trauma suddenly becomes too overwhelming.

There is the occasional phenomenon where a PCL directed at pleasure moments will instead trigger associated thoughts of loss, *&tc*. Although a *Seeker* doesn't want to get into a habit of *withdrawing* from such *reactivity* without handling it, the *process* only works by completing the PCL, and not diverting *attention* each time a *distraction* arises. We have practiced this already. If it happens, simply acknowledge that it exists and take it up in a later *process* or *session*.

ANALYTICAL RECALL

"Analytical Recall" processing is one of the first methods developed for applying our philosophy. At first, a *Seeker* needs only to *recall* or "remember" some aspect that the PCL calls for and then notice something about it.

As a *Seeker* becomes more experienced with *subjective processing* they will be in the habit of spotting various *"facets"* of a memory with these *processes*. These *facets* might include: time of day; location; living things present; emotions felt; any data sensed, such as smells, the quality of light, humidity—the list goes on.

There are four *processes* below. Each *process* consists of three PCL. These are *run* repetitively as an alternating cycle (1, 2, 3, 1, 2, 3...) until you feel good about doing the *process*. Then end the *session*, or go to

the next *process*. When first practicing, focus on just spotting specific "times" and
"people" (and any *terminals* of significant
"*mass*," such as a building, *&tc*).

Communication:

1. *"Remember a time when you enjoyed
talking to someone."*

2. *"Remember a time when someone enjoyed
talking to you."*

3. *"Remember a time when you saw two
people enjoy talking to each other."*

Agreement:

1. *"Remember a time when you agreed with
someone."*

2. *"Remember a time when someone agreed
with you."*

3. *"Remember a time when you saw two
people agree with each other."*

Liking:

1. *"Remember a time when you liked
someone."*

2. *"Remember a time when someone liked you."*

3. *"Remember a time when you saw two people like each other."*

Understanding:

1. *"Remember a time when you felt that you really understood someone."*

2. *"Remember a time when you felt that someone really understood you."*

3. *"Remember a time when you felt two other people really understood each other."*

The Systemology Professional Course
continues in the next lesson booklet:
CLEAR COMMUNICATION

APPENDIX: BETA-AWARENESS SCALE

4.0 SELF-HONESTY (BETA)
3.9 "Vibrant" ("Charismatic")
3.8 "Enthusiastic" ("In Love")
3.7 "Energetic"
3.6 "Cheerful"
3.5 CONFIDENT ("Positive")
3.4 "Determined"
3.3 "Eager"
3.2 "Alert" ("Attentive")
3.1 "Strong Interest"
3.0 INTERESTED ("Content")
2.9 "Small Interest"
2.8 "Encouraged"
2.7 "Disinterested"
2.6 "Doubtful"
2.5 INDIFFERENT ("Tolerant")
2.4 "Bored"
2.3 "Dislike" ("Neglectful")
2.2 "Tired"
2.1 "Monotony"

2.0 INVALIDATING ("Pessimistic")
1.9 "Antagonism"
1.8 "Suffering" ("In Pain")
1.7 "Confrontational"
1.6 "Violent"
1.5 ANGRY ("Negative")
1.4 "Hateful"
1.3 "Spiteful"
1.2 "Resentment"
1.1 "Anxiety"
1.0 FEAR ("Afraid")
0.9 "Terror"
0.8 "Numb"
0.7 "Evasive"
0.6 "Loss"
0.5 GRIEF ("Sadness")
0.4 "Depression"
0.3 "Victimization"
0.2 "Hopelessness"
0.1 "Apathy" ("Unconsciousness")
0.0 BETA CONTINUITY (Organic Death)

GLOSSARY

actualization : to make actual, not just potential; to bring into full solid Reality; to realize fully in *Awareness* as a "thing."

agreement (reality) : unanimity of opinion of what is "thought" to be known; an accepted arrangement of how things are; things we consider as "real" or as an "is" of "reality"; a consensus of what is real as made by standard-issue (common) participants; what an individual contributes to or accepts as "real"; in *Systemology*, a synonym for *"reality."*

alpha : the first, primary, basic, superior or beginning of some form; in *Systemology*, referring to the state of existence operating on spiritual archetypes and postulates, will and intention "exterior" to the low-level condensation and solidarity of energy and matter as the 'physical universe' (*beta*).

alpha-spirit : a "spiritual" *Life*-form; the "true" *Self* or I-AM; the *individual*; the spiritual (*alpha*) *Self* that is animating the (*beta*) physical body or *"genetic vehicle"* using a continuous *Lifeline* of spiritual ("*ZU*") energy; an individual spiritual (*alpha*) entity possessing no physical mass or measurable waveform (motion) in the Physical Universe as itself, so it animates the (*beta*) physical body or "*genetic vehicle*" as a catalyst to experience *Self*-determined causality in effect within the *Physical Universe*; a singular unit or point of *Spiritual Awareness* that is *Aware* that it is *Aware*.

ascension : actualized *Awareness* elevated to the point of true "spiritual existence" exterior to *beta existence*. An "Ascended Master" is one who has returned to an incarnation on Earth as an inherently *Enlightened One*, demonstrable in their words and actions; they have the ability to *Self-direct* the "Mind" and "Body" as *Self* (as a "Spirit"); and to maintain consciousness as a personal identity continuum with the same *Self-directed* control and communication of Will-Intention that is exercised, actualized and developed deliberately during one's present incarnation.

associative knowledge : significance or meaning of a facet or aspect assigned to (or considered to have) a direct relationship with another facet; to connect or relate ideas or facets of existence with one another; in traditional systems logic, an equivalency of significance or meaning between facets or sets that are grouped together, such as in *(a + b) + c = a + (b + c)*; in Systemology, erroneous associative knowledge is assignment of the same value to all facets or parts considered as related (even when they are not actually so), such as in *a = a, b = a, c = a* and so forth without distinction.

attention : active use of *Awareness* toward a specific aspect or thing; the act of "attending" with the presence of *Self*; a direction of focus or concentration of *Awareness* along a particular channel or conduit or toward a particular terminal node or communication termination point; the Self-directed concentration of personal energy as a combination of observation, thought-waves and consideration; focused application of *Self-Directed Awareness*.

awareness : the highest sense of-and-as *Self* in knowing and being as I-AM (the *Alpha-Spirit*); the extent of beingness directed as a viewpoint (POV) experienced by *Self* as knowingness.

beta (existence) : all manifestation in the "Physical Universe" (KI, in *Zuism*); the conditions of *Awareness* for the *Alpha-spirit* (*Self*) as a physical organic *Lifeform* or "*genetic vehicle*" in which it experiences causality in the *Physical Universe*.

charge : to fill or furnish with a quality; to supply with energy; to lay a command upon; in *Systemology*—to imbue with intention; to overspread with emotion; personal energy stores and significances entwined as fragmentation in mental images, reactive-response encoding and intellectual (and/or) programmed beliefs.

communication : successful transmission of information, data, energy (&tc.) along a message line, with a reception of feedback; an energetic flow of intention to cause an effect (or duplication) at a distance; the personal energy moved or acted upon by will or else 'selective directed attention'; the 'messenger action' used to transmit and receive energy across a medium; also relay of energy, a message or signal—or even locating a personal POV (viewpoint) for the Self—along the *ZU-line*.

confront : to come around in front of; to be in the presence of; to stand in front of, or in the face of; to meet "face-to-face" or "face-up-to"; additionally, in *Systemology*, to fully tolerate or acceptably withstand an encounter with a particular manifestation or encounter.

defragmentation : the *reparation* of wholeness; collecting all dispersed parts to reform an original whole; a process of removing "*fragmentation*" in data or knowledge to provide a clear understanding; applying techniques and processes that promote a *holistic* interconnected *alpha* state, favoring observational *Awareness* of continuity in all spiritual and physical systems; in *Systemology*, a "*Seeker*" achieving actualized "*Self-Honest Awareness*" is said to be in a basic state of *beta-defragmentation*, whereas *Alpha-defragmentation* is the rehabilitation of the *creative ability*, managing the *Spiritual Timeline* and the POV of *Self* as Alpha-Spirit (I-AM).

fragmentation : breaking into parts and scattering the pieces; the *fractioning* of wholeness or the *fracture* of a holistic interconnected *alpha* state, favoring observational *Awareness* of perceived connectivity between parts; *discontinuity*; separation of a totality into parts; in *Systemology*, a person outside of *Self-Honesty* is said to be operating from a *fragmented* state.

flow : movement across (or through) a channel (or conduit); a direction of active energetic motion, typically distinguished as either an *in-flow*, *out-flow* or *cross-flow*.

genetic-vehicle : a physical *Life*-form; the physical (*beta*) body that is animated/controlled by the (*Alpha*) *Spirit* using a continuous *Spiritual Lifeline* (ZU); a physical (*beta*) organic receptacle and catalyst for the (*Alpha*) *Self* to operate "causes" and experience "effects" within the *Physical Universe*.

holistic : the examination of interconnected systems as encompassing something greater than the *sum* of their "parts."

Human Condition : a standard default state of Human experience that is generally accepted to be the extent of its potential identity (*beingness*) —currently treated as *Homo Sapiens Sapiens,* but which is scheduled for replacement by *Homo Novus* (the "New Human").

imprint : to strongly impress, stamp, mark (or outline) onto a softer 'impressible' substance; to mark with pressure onto a surface; in *Systemology,* the term is used to indicate permanent Reality impressions marked by frequencies, energies or interactions experienced during periods of emotional distress, pain, unconsciousness, loss, enforcement, or something antagonistic to physical (personal) survival, all of which are are stored with other reactive response-mechanisms at lower-levels of *Awareness* as opposed to the active memory database and proactive processing center of the Mind; an experiential "memory-set" that may later resurface—be triggered or stimulated artificially—as Reality, of which similar responses will be engaged automatically; holographic-like imagery "stamped" onto consciousness as composed of energetic *facets* tied to the "snap-shot" of an experience.

pilot : a professional steersman responsible for healthy functional operation of a ship toward a specific destination; in *Systemology*, an intensive trained individual qualified to specially apply *Systemology Processing* to assist other *Seekers* on the *Pathway*.

presence : the quality of some thing (energy/matter) being "present" in space-time; personal orientation of *Self* as an *Awareness* (*POV*) located in present space-time (environment) and communicating with extant energy-matter.

processing command line (PCL) or **command line** : a directed input; a specific command using highly selective language for *Systemology Processing*; a predetermined directive statement (cause) intended to focus concentrated attention (effect).

processing, systematic : the inner-workings or "through-put" result of systems; in *Systemology*, a method of applied spiritual technology used toward personal Self-Actualization; methods of selective directed attention, communicated language and associative imagery that increases personal control of the human condition.

realization : the clear perception of an understanding; a consideration or understanding on what is "actual"; to make "real" or give "reality" to so as to grant a property of "being-ness" or "being as it is"; the state or instance of coming to an *Awareness*; in *Systemology*, "gnosis" or true knowledge achieved during *systematic processing*; achievement of a new (or "higher") cognition, true knowledge or perception of Self; a consideration of reality or assignment of meaning.

responsibility : the *ability* to *respond*; the extent of mobilizing *power* and *understanding* an individual maintains as *Awareness* to enact *change*; the proactive ability to *Self-direct* and make decisions independent of an outside authority.

Seeker : an individual on the *Pathway to Self-Honesty*; a practitioner of *Mardukite Systemology* or *Systemology Processing*, that is working toward *Spiritual Ascension*.

Self-actualization : bringing the full potential of the Human spirit into Reality; expressing full capabilities and creativeness of the *Alpha-Spirit*.

Self-determinism : the freedom to act, clear of external control or influence; the personal control of Will to direct intention.

Self-honesty : the basic or original *alpha* state of *being* and *knowing*; clear and present total

Awareness of-and-as *Self*, in its most basic and true proactive expression of itself as *Spirit* or *I-AM*—free of artificial attachments, perceptive filters and other emotionally-reactive or mentally-conditioned programming imposed on the human condition by the systematized physical world; the ability to experience existence without judgment.

spiritual timeline : a continuous stream of moment-to-moment *Mental Images* (or a record of experiences) that defines the "past" of a spiritual being (or *Alpha-Spirit*) and which includes impressions (*imprints, &tc.*) from all life-incarnations and significant spiritual events the being has encountered; in Systemology, also "*backtrack.*"

Systemology : a modern tradition of applied religious philosophy and spiritual technology based on *Arcane Tablets* (in combination with "*general systemology*" and "*games theory*") developed in the New Age underground by Joshua Free in 2011 as an advanced futurist extension of the *Mardukite Research Org.*; also known as "*Mardukite Systemology,*" "*Metahuman Systemology*" and "*Spiritual Systemology.*"

terminal (node) : a point, end, or mass, on a line; a connection point for closing an electric circuit, such as a post on a battery terminating at each end of its own systematic function; a point of connectivity with other points; in systems, a contact point of interaction; a point of interaction with other points.

turbulence : a quality or state of distortion or disturbance that creates irregularity of a flow or pattern; the quality or state of aberration on a line (such as ragged edges) or the emotional "turbulent feelings" attached to a particular flow or terminal node; a violent, haphazard or disharmonious commotion (such as in the ebb of gusts and lulls of wind action).

ZU : the ancient Sumerian cuneiform sign for the archaic verb—"*to know,*" "*knowingness*" or "*awareness*"; in *Mardukite Zuism and Systemology*, the active energy/matter of the "Spiritual Universe" (AN) experienced as a *Lifeforce* or *consciousness* that imbues living forms extant in the "Physical Universe" (KI); "*Spiritual Life Energy*"; energy demonstrated by the WILL of an actualized *Alpha-Spirit* in the "Spiritual Universe" (AN), which impinges its *Awareness* into the Physical Universe (KI), animating/controlling *Life* for its experience of *beta-existence* along an individual Alpha-Spirit's personal *Identity-continuum*, called a *ZU-line*.

Zu-**Line** : a theoretical construct in *Mardukite*

83

Zuism and Systemology demonstrating *Spiritual Life Energy* (ZU) as a personal individual "continuum" of Awareness interacting with all Spheres of Existence on the Standard Model of Systemology; a spectrum of potential variations and interactions of a monistic continuum or singular *Spiritual Life Energy (ZU)* demonstrated on the Standard Model; an energetic channel of potential POV and "locations" of Beingness, demonstrated in early Systemology materials as an individual Alpha-Spirit's personal *Identity-continuum*, potentially connecting *Awareness (ZU)* of *Self* with "*Infinity*" simultaneous with all points considered in existence; a symbolic demonstration of the "*Life-line*" on which *Awareness (ZU)* extends from the direction of the "Spiritual Universe" (AN) in its true original *alpha state* through an entire possible range of activity resulting in its *beta state* and control of a *genetic-entity* occupying the *Physical Universe (KI)*.

Fundamentals of Systemology
in six
Basic Course Lesson Booklets

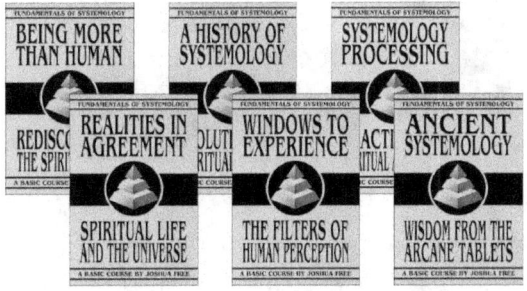

Also
available
as a
six-in-one
hardcover
edition!

THE SYSTEMOL

Seekers and students of the *Basic Course* and *Professional Course* will also be interested in the *Advanced Series* of the *Systemology Core*. These volumes are a complete chronological record of the Mardukite New Thought developments from the Systemology Society, published in 2019 through 2023.

The *Systemology Core* begins with the first professional publication released when the *Mardukite Systemology Society* emerged from the underground in 2019, with: *"The Tablets of Destiny Revelation."*

OGY PATHWAY

The Tablets of Destiny Revelation:
How Long-Lost Anunnaki Wisdom
Can Change the Fate of Humanity

Crystal Clear: *Handbook for Seekers*

Metahuman Destinations (2 *volumes*)

Imaginomicon:
Approaching Gateways to Higher Universes

Way of the Wizard: *Utilitarian Systemology*

Systemology-180: *Fast-Track to Ascension*

Systemology Backtrack:
Reclaiming Spiritual Power & Past-Life Memory

PUBLISHED BY THE **JOSHUA FREE** IMPRINT REPRESENTING

The Mardukite Academy of Systemology

THE JOSHUA FREE IMPRINT
JFI PUBLICATIONS

MARDUKITE
ZUISM

mardukite.com

www.ingramcontent.com/pod-product-compliance
Lightning Source LLC
Chambersburg PA
CBHW071214120626
46546CB00006B/2556